Prayer for Jesus and other poems

by

Elaine Day

Published by Feather Books
Shrewsbury SY3 OBW, U.K.
Tel/fax; 01743 872177

e-mail: john@jjwfeather.co.uk

ISBN: 1 84175 028 X

First Published 2000
Reprinted   2012

No. 101 in the Feather Books Poetry Series

CONTENTS

	page
Prayer for Jesus	5
Jesus	6
Joy to the World	7
From heaven you came	8
Come, dearest Jesus	9
Praise Jesus, the King of Glory	10
On Christmas Night	11
I love you, O Lord	12
How lovely is your dwelling place	13
How firm his foundation	14
I will sing	14
Jesus our Saviour	15
Jesus, Stand Among us	16
I believe in Jesus	16
A crown with many crowns	17
Who Do You Say I Am?	18
PRAYER	19
Heaven	20
Eternal depth	21
We have a gospel to proclaim	22

Low in the Grave	23
The glory of the king	24
We give God thanks	25
Let us with a gladdened mind	26
God's Greatest Word	27
I hear a voice calling	28
Dear Father	29
Hear me, Oh shepherd of Israel	30
I Know inside my redeemer lives	31
I place into your hands	32
Preserve Me Oh god	33
Father, hear our prayer	34
Spirit of God	35
Jesus Christ, Holy Christ	36
You are God and we praise you	37
The voice of God	38
I heard a voice	39
In the Snow-filled universe	40
Jesus is my Saviour	41
On the eve of Christmas	42
He's our king	43
Jesus, my truth, my way	44

PRAYER FOR JESUS

Jesus, in your name, I go
My daily labour to amend;
You, only you, resolved to know,
On you, alone, Lord, I depend.

My task, your wisdom has assigned
Jesus let me my life fulfil;
In all I do, your presence find,
To prove your good and perfect will.

Jesus, may I sit at your right hand,
Your eyes, my eyes gaze at lovingly
And labouring on at your command,
I offer all my life to you.

Jesus, let me understand
Every moment, praise and pray;
You still the things hate creates,
And bring around another day.

JESUS

Open my eyes, Jesus.
I want to see you,
To reach out and touch you,
To say, "I love you."
Open my heart, Lord.
I want to touch you,
To feel each beat,
Each pulsating breath,
To love you for ever.

Open my ears, Jesus.
I want to hear you,
To listen to each
Word you speak,
To understand now
And for ever.
                        Amen.

JOY TO THE WORLD

Joy to the World,
Jesus has risen!
A halo of bright light shines
In the almighty heaven;
Jesus the name above all
In the Lord's heaven.
Come to us
And sing with us,
Your praises as we pray.

Chorus.
Joy to the world
And to every nation!
Lift up your hearts
So that he can hear
Your happy songs
Up in heaven.

Joy to the world!
And in love adoring
Who with perfect wisdom,
Came to live with us all,
God who sent his Son
So that we can live
A happy life,
A fulfilled one,
One day up in heaven.

FROM HEAVEN YOU CAME

From heaven you came,
O, glorious Lord,
To take away our sin;
Wash clean our souls
To uplift us in your glory,
To hold us up high,
To love the people on earth,
To revel in your glory.

There in his garden of Gethsemane
Our heavy load he chose to bear,
His heart was heavy with sorrow
As he listened to our prayers;
His hands bore the scars of nails
As we worshipped at his feet.
'Forgive us Lord, we have sinned.
Take away our pain.'

COME, DEAREST JESUS

Come, dearest Jesus, descend and dwell
By gracious love to live inside us all;
Then we shall know the power of your love,
The joy inside our hearts.

Come, fill our lives with heavenly love,
Make our world a better place,
And teach us to serve you,
So that we may live in peace.

Now to the Lord whose power is great,
We sing our praises forevermore
Be everlasting in our hearts,
Bring with you a joyous heart.

Chorus.
He lives,
He lives,
Hallelujah!
For he is King
Over all the earth!

PRAISE JESUS, THE KING OF GLORY

Praise Jesus, the king of glory;
to his feet my troubles come,
pain and suffering,
healing, glory,
to the Lord my praise I sing.

Alleluia, Alleluia,
to the Lord my praise I sing!

Praise Jesus for his grace and love
to our children in great need,
praise him uphold him,
now and for ever,
slow to catch the forbidden fruit.

Alleluia, Alleluia,
To the Lord my praise I sing!

Praise the Angels that surround him,
way up high in heaven above;
praise him for his tender mercies,
swift to bless, and slow to scorn.

Alleluia, Alleluia,
to the Lord my praise I sing!

ON CHRISTMAS NIGHT

On Christmas night
We sing his praises
Up to the Angels
In heaven above;
For he has the glory
And the knowledge,
He died for us
To take away sin.

Then why on Earth are we sad?
Let us rejoice
In the great Noel;
Praise and Worship
Our dear Lord above,
Who died for us
To take away sin.

Chorus
For he is kind
And he is good,
The great Noel
Of mankind.

Out of the darkness
Came our dear Lord,
Which made the angels
Sing and rejoice:
"Glory to God in the highest.
Peace on Earth
And in heaven above."

I LOVE YOU, O LORD

I love you, O Lord,
For you are a tower of strength.
The cords of the grave
They do not hold me,
for I'm with you
In your Kingdom come.

I Love you , O Lord,
For you have saved me.
You brought me to a place of liberty
And rescued me
From mortal sin.

Chorus
I love you, my Lord,
For you have saved me.
You have saved me,
You have saved me,
I love you, O Lord,
For you have saved me,
You have saved me.

HOW LOVELY IS YOUR DWELLING PLACE

How lovely is your dwelling place,
The peace that surrounds us,
The love that overflows within you,
That does enrich our hearts.

Chorus
Come, O Saviour, and behold us,
Live within us for evermore,
Raise up our arms,
Lift up our spirits,
Be within for evermore.

How lovely is your dwelling place,
Blessed are those that praise you,
For your love is so great,
Your heart so pure,
Indeed you are true,
Until the end.

Chorus
Come, O Saviour, and behold us,
Live within us for evermore,
Raise up our arms,
Lift up our spirits,
Be within us for evermore.

HOW FIRM HIS FOUNDATION

How firm his foundation,
The glory of the Lord,
As strong as an ox,
As great as his refuge;
He holds us
And he tends us,
To shape and caress us,
As our lives go on.

How firm his foundation,
When in heaven we arise
To sit at his right hand,
And listen to his stories;
To say the great Hallelujah!
To our Lord and King,
To rise from the ashes,
And to be as one with Him.

I WILL SING

I will sing the praises
Of my wonderful King,
How he left the earth
To rise up to his Lord;
He came back to save us,
He died for our sins,
Yes, I'll sing the wondrous songs,
That indeed makes him King.

I was lost, but he found me
Forlorn and bitter,
And cold right through;
But his heart gave me gladness,
His arms held me close,
Days of darkness are now long gone;
As Jesus lives
I will sing.

JESUS OUR SAVIOUR

Jesus our Saviour,
You stand among us
In light inaccessible
That blinds our eyes;
Most blessed, most glorious,
The King of Kings,
You stand among us
To take away sin.

Loving and caring
And silent as night,
Teach us to love you
And throw away sin;
We blossom and flourish
As you only know,
Teach us to love you
And grow evermore.

JESUS, STAND AMONG US

Jesus, you come before us
In your risen power,
To enthrone us and rejoice,
Our hallowed King.

Breathe the Holy Spirit
Into every heart,
Take away the fears and sorrows
That make us sin.

Then with gladdened footsteps
We'll follow you,
Listening to each and every word
From you, our glorious King.

I BELIEVE IN JESUS

I believe in Jesus,
Who created heaven and earth;
Source of light and wisdom,
bringing light and power to earth.

I believe in God the Saviour,
The Father of mankind;
Who was crucified for us
To wash away our sins.

I believe in the Holy Spirit,
Inspirer of heaven and earth;
A pledge that we inherit
To fulfil our lives on earth.

Then honour, glory and exalt
The great Lord's name on high
He that cleanses us of sin
That we may draw more nigh.

A CROWN WITH MANY CROWNS

A crown with many crowns
Wears our Lord Jesus;
Hark, how the angels sing
To our risen Lord;
Of him who died for us
To cast away our sins;
A great God and King,
Whose crown has many crowns.

Crown him the Lord of life,
A man so holy and eternal;
Crown him the King of creation
Who lives that death may die;
For he died for us,
Rose for us,
To be our eternal king;
A crown with many crowns
Wears our great God and King.

WHO DO YOU SAY I AM?

'Who do you say I am'? said he,
Raising his eyes up above;
His friends knew, without doubt
That he was their friend of love.

'Who do you say I am?' said he
Using the gifts he possessed;
To love thousands, and everyone knew
That he was the creator of joy.

'Who do you say I am?' said he
Stilling a storm, a tidal wave,
To make a great calm so they knew
That he was indeed peace.

'Who do you say I am?' said he,
Gently holding a child;
He was great, yet our brother revealing
He was so meek and mild.

'Who do you say I am?' said he,
As the pathway of gladness he trod;
And we replied, 'Thou art our Lord,
The Son of the living God.'

PRAYER

Some tell us that prayer is in the mind,
But for me, it is in the heart.
Is prayer the only result,
Only comfort we find?
That God does not answer? But answer he does.
I have knelt down in his church
And I have received.
My faith has grown stronger,
And my love deeper.
I have seen God reach down
From heaven above,
Reach out his arms
In the quiet solitude.
He has moved mountains,
Touched each and every person.
We know God. He works miracles.
He works in a wonderful way.
So reach out and touch Him,
He is just waiting for you…
To touch Him.

HEAVEN

Up in heaven I see stars,
Stars and a fountain;
Peace and serenity cover this land,
The people smile
And feel no pain;
Where once there was pain,
Agony and torment
Now there's only peace.
I'd like to go to heaven,
See my Maker and the others,
Sing in eternal bliss,
Play a harp,
Wear a long robe,
Fear no evil,
Because there is none.
Up in heaven I sense peace,
Serenity…and an eternal bed.

ETERNAL DEPTH

Eternal depth of love divine
Shield us from our sins;
Hold us in your loving arms,
Enrich us with your love.

Mould us and caress us,
Each and every one,
For love is eternal
And life is bliss;
How bright your light shines
Over all the Earth!

We hide beneath your shadow,
Our flesh, soul, spirit
Come to you.
Lord in heaven,
Protect us
As we come to love you
Each and every day.

Eternal depth of love divine,
How wide your healing power;
Fire us with full love for You,
Fill our hearts for evermore.

WE HAVE A GOSPEL TO PROCLAIM

We have a gospel to proclaim,
Good news for everyone
Jesus Christ has risen,
Ascended up to heaven.

Tell of his birth in Israel,
Not born in hall or house;
But born to be a King
In a stable all so bare.

Tell of his death on the cross,
Salvation for us all;
That we may live in heaven
As Jesus ordained for us.

Now we rejoice to name him King,
Our crosses He often bears;
Our sins are on his shoulders,
Our troubles we shall tell to him.

LOW IN THE GRAVE

Low in the grave he lay,
Our loving Lord the King;
To rise again living,
To come among us
As our friend.

We rolled the stone away,
Away from his tomb,
To find no sign
Of our Lord,
Except the clothes that lay
On stone that wrapped our loving King.

Death cannot hold him in,
For he rises among us,
To be for ever in our midst;
To be in glory above all others,
Our loving Lord and King.

For we sing our praises
To our Lord and King;
Death cannot hold him
Our Lord, Saviour and King,
The one, the only one,
Jesus Christ!

THE GLORY OF THE KING

The glory of the King was seen
'Alleluia to the King!';
For he reigns on high
Our most loving Lord,
Our Saviour always on high,
And people ran and waved and cheered,
'Hallelujah to our King most high!'

The glory of the King was seen
Around the universe;
For he made the plants, the people
And the animals and birds;
The very air we breathe and live by.
So praise the Lord,
The chosen one;
Praise him with great adulation,
For he is always with us,
At our sleep, and at our play.
He knows our wrongs,
He knows our rights,
For he is human,
He is the King.

WE GIVE GOD THANKS

We give God thanks
for all we do,
for all we see,
from this day on,
to worship him,
and to adore;
We give God thanks
for all we do.

We give God thanks
for the birds and bees,
for uplifting us,
to Himself on high,
for taking away our sins.

We give God thanks
for all our skills;
Jesus' hands how they reach out
to those who suffer long,
to help the anxious and the ill.
We give God thanks.   Amen.

LET US WITH A GLADDENED MIND

Let us with a gladdened mind
Rejoice, the Lord is King!
He came to save us,
To take away our sin,
For his mercies will endure,
Ever faithful, ever sure.

Let us with a gladdened mind,
Be filled with love anew
By him our Lord up above,
Who came to rule the earth,
For he came to save us,
To gladden each and every heart;
Let us with a gladdened mind,
Rejoice, the Lord is King!

Let us with a gladdened mind,
Praise the Lord, for he is kind;
He shows us the way,
Leads us from the grave
Into his holy place,
Where there is peace
And a restful bed.

GOD'S GREATEST WORD

It was like a breath of fresh air,
God's greatest Word;
For he gave to us his only Son,
Jesus.
Born of Mary,
He died for our sins,
He gave us life,
Jesus.
Who loves everybody,
A light in the darkness,
A heavenly Being
Declaring
God's greatest Word.
Let the words of the Almighty
Overwhelm my soul,
My life,
My all.
                                        Amen.

I HEAR A VOICE CALLING

I hear a voice calling
Somewhere in the distance,
A man's voice,
So loud,
So proud,
Rejoicing his good news.
I cannot yet see him,
But he's drawing near.
He sounds happy,
So eager to please,
His love is overflowing,
I know not why.
I guess he's young,
Not old and grey,
Proud enough to stand tall,
A manly man.
But I'm so short,
So stout and fat,
Not like him;
Though short and lame,
Through Him I'm glad to be alive.

DEAR FATHER

Dear Father, your love is wonderful,
Your heart is kind and pure,
Your hands are gentle, your face is kind;
I reach out and touch You,
Hear your voice.
You draw me in with loving kindness,
You lift me up to a great height,
However deep that I may sink;
You pull me back to your great side,
However far that I may wander;
You follow me
And lead me back
To your chosen path,
The path of truth;
And even when I plunge
Into greater depths,
You raise me up again.
Dear Father,
Thank you for being just You,
For sheltering me
And all your sheep;
So that we can rest in your presence
In your everlasting love
And in such great kindness
That only You can show.   Amen.

HEAR ME, OH SHEPHERD OF ISRAEL

Hear me, Oh ,Shepherd of Israel
You that lead your flock to pasture
You that are enthroned upon high
Before Man, Beseech me
Your kingdom come, forevermore

Hear me, Oh Shepherd of Israel
You have fed us with your love
You endow us with your wisdom
You have cried tears over us
Through your undying love

Hear me, Oh Shepherd of Israel
Restore in us the faith of God
Enrich our souls with your peace
Like the Doves that fly up high
Gracious as your love

You cleared the ground before us
You enriched our souls
You raised our hearts
So that there is peace
And harmony
Forevermore

I KNOW INSIDE MY REDEEMER LIVES

I know inside my redeemer lives,
My heart sings out his songs;
By his love and everlasting love,
He shines inside my heart.

May the Word of God grow inside,
In our cold and heartless hearts;
Fill us up with love anew
And redeem us from Satan.

Lord, that we may learn from You
To walk your path of righteousness;
Come, Father, teach us how to pray
And live inside *your* heart.

Take our boasted wisdom spoiled,
Weak and helpless as a child's;
Bring instead the truth of righteousness
So that we all may walk in your light.
                                    Amen.

I PLACE INTO YOUR HANDS

I place into your hands
All of the things I cannot do:
All of my sin,
And my life,
To show me the way that I must go.
For I know I can trust You,
Honour You,
Adore you;
So I place in your hands
My life,
My all.

I place into your hands
All of my fears and anxieties;
I love to sing your praises
To you, our beloved King;
Father, I want to speak the words
That made you great and holy;
Father, I want to love again,
So make my life whole and worthy.

I place into your hands
And do the things You want me to;
To speak the same language
That you speak to me;
For I know that I'm at one with You,
In your loving arms,
That you are speaking;
And everyone listens
To your great wisdom through the Word.

PRESERVE ME OH GOD

Preserve me, O God,
For in you I have taken refuge;
Anoint me,
Caress me,
Uplift me
In your arms.

Preserve me, O God,
Feed me with your love,
For I have sinned;
Against all odds
Anoint me with your love.

I have said to the Lord,
'All my good depends on You.
You are He in whom I trust,
Anoint me with your love.'

Preserve me, O God,
And I will bless your Name;
My heart is glad,
My spirit rejoices,
That I am at one with God.

FATHER, HEAR OUR PRAYER

Father, hear our prayer
In times of need and good,
When we are hurting,
When we are too proud,
Father, hear our prayer.

Father, hear our prayer,
In times of happiness and lowliness,
For when we sin,
It is with terrible sorrow,
And we come to you for forgiveness.

Not for ever in green pastures
Do we want to walk,
But to be at your side,
From this day on
Now and for evermore.

Be our strength in times of weakness,
Be our salvation in times of anger,
Be always there at our side,
Father, hear our prayer.
Amen.

SPIRIT OF GOD

Spirit of God, descend upon me,
Take hold of my heart
Through all my pulses move;
Strengthen my weaknesses,
Mighty as you are,
No sudden rendering,
As my feet are of clay.

I ask for no dream,
For I have nothing to hold me;
Spirit of God, descend upon me,
No angel visiting
I deserve;
Save first my soul
From this torn heart.

Spirit of God, descend upon me;
Teach me to feel that you are real
And make me love you as I should;
Spirit of God,
Descend upon me.
                            Amen.

JESUS CHRIST, HOLY CHRIST

Jesus Christ, Holy Christ,
Came to Earth, God had blessed
Mary and Joseph came from birth
To be with him until the end.
Sleep in heavenly rest,
Sleep in heavenly rest.

Jesus Christ, Holy Christ,.
What can I give him
My dear Saviour?
For he died for our sins,
Took away pain,
Our mortal sins.
Sleep in heavenly rest,
Sleep in heavenly rest.

Jesus Christ, Holy Christ,
Many times he has blessed,
Gave us shelter from the storms,
He gave us his heart
and undying love.
Sleep in heavenly rest,
Sleep in heavenly rest.

YOU ARE GOD AND WE PRAISE YOU

You are God and we praise You,
Our eternal light at the end of the day;
All of mankind worships you,
Our loving Lord, Jesus Christ.

You are God and we praise You,
Our God, the King of glory;
You enrich our lives,
Take hold of our hearts,
You whom all the angels adore.

You are God and we praise You,
King of all glory;
You overcame the pain of death,
Rose from the poverty of earth
Into the riches of heaven.

Come then, Lord, help us decide
On the path of righteousness,
Be with us in heaven
Or deep down below,
Or walking on the earth with You.
Now and forever more.   Amen.

THE VOICE OF GOD

The voice of God goes round the world,
His glory speaks itself;
The great King heralds
His triumphant return
To the garden of Eden.
He goes within
From star to star,
Country to country,
A light for every nation,
Colour and creed.
Anointed with the spirit,
Three in One,
I shall praise him:
"Glory to the King!"
No broken Angel shall ever sing,
But an uplifting voice shall be heard
From kingdom to kingdom,
Planet to planet;
The blind shall see,
The lame will walk,
And prisoners will laugh in joy
At their freedom.
For God is with everyone
In our hearts and in our minds.
So,
The voice of God goes round the world
His glory speaks for itself.

I HEARD A VOICE

I heard a voice
The voice of Jesus
Saying to me,
'Seek and you shall find.'
The voice of Jesus,
So loud,
So Clear,
Promising me many things
If I try so hard.
I felt his head upon my breast,
His gentle voice so quiet, so proud,
Telling me all my darkest sins,
That I have ever encountered.
I find Jesus in my resting place,
My home, my garden,
Just like his;
Not with a stone that tried to hold him,
But a garden, just like mine.
I heard a voice
The voice of Jesus
Saying to me,
'Seek and you shall find.'

IN THE SNOW-FILLED UNIVERSE

In the snow-filled universe
That Jesus Christ made true
Came the baby Jesus
Laid out on his bed;
For he shines round the world,
Lighting up the skies
In the snow-filled universe
That Jesus Christ made true.

For he is my Saviour,
My Beholder, Lord and King;
He gives us blessings
Of many, many things;
He shows in infinite wisdom
Of every blessed thing
In the snow-filled universe
That Jesus Christ made true.

Our God in heaven adores us,
He lights up our world
To give to us, receive us
From the sinners world,
For he knows our failures.
Without doubt there are many
In the snow-filled universe
That Jesus Christ made true.

JESUS IS MY SAVIOUR

Jesus is my Saviour
For he reigns on high,
To take me in his arms,
Protecting me
And all I do;
For he is the Anointed One,
Honest, down to earth and true;
He shows us mercy
In everything we do;
He does not bear us grudges,
He takes away our sin,
To free us from all tyranny
And to cleanse us in all things;
Jesus is my Saviour
For he reigns on high,
Protecting me
And in everything I do.

ON THE EVE OF CHRISTMAS

On the eve of Christmas
In a stable bare
Laid the dear Lord Jesus
With Mary, oh so rare;
For she loved him
And she cared,
Gave her heart so glad
On the eve of Christmas
In a stable bare.

On the eve of Christmas
At the inn did shepherds come,
They found him with the cattle
Laid in swaddling clothes.
On this happy morning
Come let us adore him,
Who came to us at Christmas
In a stable bare.

HE'S OUR KING

He is our King
And our salvation;
God sent him down
To be with us;
For his good deeds
We shall praise him;
He made us believe
That good is good,
For in his heart
We all shall see
The good in him
From heaven above.

He is kind,
And we worship
All the things
That he made good;
He takes away sin
And we adore him;
He brings in the good
And takes away the sin;
For he is kind
And he is mild,
Loving Jesus,
Saviour of mankind.

JESUS, MY TRUTH, MY WAY

Jesus, my truth, my way.
On his shoulders he does bear
My cross of sin.
He is my glad rejoicing,
And I proclaim to all
He is King!

Let Jesus be my wisdom, my guide,
My Counsellor, my strength;
Oh, leave me not,
Stay at my side,
Now and for evermore,
From this day on.

Through the fire and water you bring
Forgiveness to fill my cup,
When all sin is at last destroyed.
Let me be there
At a new awakening,
At a brand new dawn.

Oh make us all like you
In strength and wisdom;
And at our new birth,
When perfected in grace,
Will we hold you
In everlasting arms.   Amen.